I0019775

HOW TO ERASE YOURSELF FROM THE INTERNET COMPLETELY

HOW TO REMAIN ANONYMOUS ONLINE

By

MOHAN J. MENON

Copyrighted Material

*Copyright © 2017 – **Valencia Publishing House***

All Rights Reserved.

No part of this publication may be reproduced, stored in a retrieval system or transmitted in any form or by any means, electronic, mechanical, photocopying, recording or otherwise without the proper written consent of the copyright holder, except brief quotations used in a review.

Published by:

www.Valenciapub.com

Valencia Publishing House
P.O. Box 548
Wilmer, Alabama 36587

Cover & Interior designed

By

Alex Lockridge

First Edition

CONTENT AT A GLANCE

PART – 1

HOW TO ERASE YOURSELF FROM THE INTERNET COMPLETELY

THE INTERNET & YOUR PERSONAL INFORMATION

THE internet, vast and virtually limitless. Millions of interconnected computers sending and receiving Petabytes of information at any given time. In this great age of the internet, keeping your identity protected is of uttermost importance.

Every time we sign into our personal email provider, download a file off the internet or even get connected to our ISPs, we are immediately vulnerable to information leaks, which can include our identity.

We put out a lot of information about ourselves online. When we sign up for an online service, our Name, date of birth, location (via our IP address) and other personally identifiable information is given out. Some of these services might not have the right measures in place to adequately secure our information. We become vulnerable to identity theft and other forms of cybercrime.

A quick online search (on one of your favorite search engines) of your name will show you how easily accessible your information is. What you posted several years ago, that embarrassing high school photograph, easily viewable by a potential employer, your future partner or a malicious cybercriminal.

When we look at the internet we can look at two broad categories:

- The surface web
- The deep web

The surface web is where most of your information is easily searchable. Your name, location, and images are visible for anyone with interest in finding more about you. Large marketing firms are consuming large swaths of information about online users and building complex personality matrices about users and selling this information to the highest bidder.

The deep web is a bit more cloaked, but information leaks do still happen at this level. This is where service providers like Facebook, twitter, google, and yahoo comes in. They hold more than just personal attributes about yourself, but they have information about who your close personal networks are, what places you frequent to, what goods and services you buy the most.

They hold the gold of information about individuals. At the deep web level, most of your data is secured for most major sites through their private policy and terms of service. But don't think they don't sell your information to a company who is willing to pay a good price for it. If you read the any of these company's terms of services, you will be shocked as to how little control you have over your personal information and how much power and control they have over your own information.

The information we really have more control over is on the surface web. We can limit the information that is available to the public by taking some cautionary steps.

There are three ways to go about erasing your digital footprint.

1. You can go about deleting all your online past from websites you have signed up for.
2. Request websites you have no control over to remove your data or suppress it.
3. Be self-disciplined. Don't let your data be re-acquired in the same way as before.

WHY WOULD YOU WANT TO ERASE YOUR DIGITAL FOOTPRINT?

TECHNOLOGY is evolving at a fast rate, and some services are only available to smartphone owners so if you don't own one, you are being left out of the digital world. Most people use the internet mainly for communication, networking, entertainment, business, education and shopping, however, social networking and shopping take up the bulk of the time that an individual spends on the internet.

In just one minute, there are 700k+ Facebook logins, 2.78 million videos are watched on YouTube, 40K+ posts are on Instagram, 350K + new tweet. Social networking has had one of the biggest impacts in society today. It has totally changed the way in which we network, keep in touch and make friends with people all over the world. The most popular platforms such as Facebook, Twitter, and Instagram are all fun ways for people to interact, share their thoughts and photos and stories.

While it's fun to share, easier to shop, get work done, catch up with friends and family, what you share and how much you share is extremely important. I'm sure you have heard this adage, the internet never forgets. You always leave behind a digital footprint. A digital footprint is the information about an individual that is on the internet because of their online activity.

There are two types of digital footprint which are passive and active. A passive footprint is made without the owner's knowledge, while an active digital footprint is created when personal data is made available intentionally by an individual e.g. by sharing personal details for social media websites, etc. Both active and passive footprints can be stored in many ways. A digital footprint can be stored in an online database. This is known as a hit. This footprint can track the users IP (Internet Protocol) address when it was created, what country they are in and the footprint later being analyzed.

Active digital footprints can also be stored in a variety of ways. When a person is online, a footprint can be stored by a user being logged into a site when making a post or change, with the registered name being connected to the edit. Both active and passive footprints can be stored as data for offline use. Digital footprints are left behind intentionally, e.g. when you are writing posts, sharing photos, etc. on your social media accounts, making purchases online. They can also be left unintentionally when you are browsing the internet.

On the World Wide Web, the digital footprint is the information left behind as a result of an individual's browsing activity and is stored as 'cookies.' Your digital footprint is extremely valuable to certain groups of people, namely, the social networking companies, potential employers, the government, marketers, and data mining companies.

Companies like Facebook, Twitter, and Google, sell your data to third parties which help them know the tastes and preferences of certain groups, demographics and with their overall marketing plan. It has now become more advanced because they have more specific data. They now know your exact location, age, etc. Have you ever liked a Facebook page for a certain product, and then all of a sudden Facebook is suggesting similar pages for you to like?

That's an example of what happens when they sell your data.

A potential employer would want to know what kind of a person you are and if you are a good fit for their company. All they need to do is conducted a simple Google search and see what information about you pops up. If you did not set strict privacy settings, a lot of information about you and what you share is easily accessible to anyone.

Government agencies are also now very interested in an individual's online activity for vetting purposes and surveillance purposes. Social networking sites record all of the activity of an individual such as social groups, location, lifestyle, etc. All in a bid to get more targeted data about certain users who are lucrative to sell to marketers who want to target their products at the individuals who are most likely to consume their goods.

A digital footprint has its disadvantages. You may be denied a job because an inappropriate photo of yourself popped in a Google search, you could be in trouble with the law enforcement agencies for sharing political views which may be perceived negatively or even worse, you may be a victim of identity theft. You may tighten your privacy settings on all your email and social media accounts. However, it still does not give you complete privacy. We are also now exposed by mass surveillance by governments which infringes on an individual's right to privacy. Big brother is always watching.

If you really want complete privacy on the internet, then the only way to succeed is by disappearing from the internet completely. This can be done by deleting all your social media and email accounts, using more discrete payment methods online, securing your smartphone or ditching it, and browsing discretely. We shall now look at all of these in detail.

CONSEQUENCES OF GOING OFF THE GRID

BEFORE you proceed with erasing yourself from the internet, you need to think about the decision very carefully before proceeding. Much of what is suggested in the book cannot be undone. This means that you will lose information, forfeit any marketable presence that you've developed online, and in some cases, you'll even lose the opportunity to restart your account using the same name or even the same email address. These are drastic measures and should be treated as such.

- Consider what is driving your wish to delete yourself completely. Is it a cyber stalker? Is it a single bad experience? Or are you just fed up with its invasiveness in your life? Be sure you fully understand the issue before diving in.

- Are there other ways around the problem, such as changing your online name or using a different email account from your normal one? For example, if your current email address has some unsavory online associations, can you create a separate one that you use purely for professional transactions like sending resumes, creating business profiles, etc.?

- Realize that you might not even remember all the sites you've joined, created, participated in, etc.

ERASING YOUR ONLINE PRESENCE

NOW THAT YOU ARE READY YOU KNOW ALL THE CAVEATS ABOUT GOING OFF THE DIGITAL GRID AND HAVE MADE UP YOUR MIND TO EASE YOUR DIGITAL FOOTPRINT WE CAN NOW GO ABOUT START TO EXPUNGE OUR DIGITAL PRESENCE FROM THE INTERNET.

DELETE OR DEACTIVATE YOUR SHOPPING, SOCIAL NETWORK, AND WEB SERVICE ACCOUNTS

Delete accounts. As already noted, it's possible that you've joined up to more sites than you'll ever remember. The more popular the site, however, the better it is to remove yourself from it when trying to disappear from the internet. This won't necessarily resolve "deep web" memory of you, but it's a good start. The following list is provided to help make it easier for you to know how to start erasing yourself from the major sites:

1. Social accounts: Including the obvious ones, such as Facebook, Twitter, LinkedIn, Instagram, Tumblr, Google+ or even MySpace?

2. Shopping accounts: Aside from the big ones, such as eBay, Amazon, Gap.com, Macys.com, do you still have public accounts on sites like Craigslist and other auction sites?

3. Game Sites

HOW TO PERMANENTLY DELETE YOUR FACEBOOK ACCOUNT

Ever since Facebook burst into the limelight back in 2006, it has been nothing short of breaking digital records. It is the world's largest social networking site, with over a billion users and over 700k+ logins per minute, you surely cannot deny its popularity. It helps us remain connected with friends, and family all over the world and is a great tool for people to connect. However, it does have its fair share of privacy concerns.

The Facebook timeline exposes your whole life to the public, from the day you were born right up to today. All your significant achievements and milestones are made visible. You can change the privacy settings on your account to make it more secure. However, that doesn't guarantee complete privacy. Your Facebook account will still pop up when someone searches for you in any of the popular search engines, e.g., Google and Bing. Facebook also collects a lot of personal data such as your location, age address, phone number email, etc. and your browsing habits which can be accessed by governments and spy agencies through mass surveillance.

The following are the steps to permanently delete your Facebook account.

Step 1

Click on the downward facing caret.

Step 2:

Click on the Settings

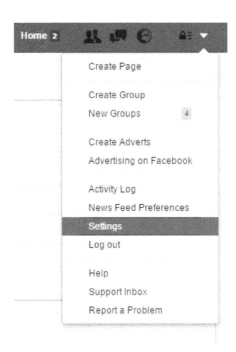

On the left most column, click on the "Security" tab

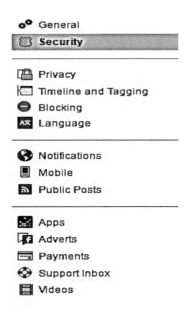

Look for "deactivate your account" at the bottom of the page.

Security Settings

Login Alerts	Get an alert when anyone logs in to your account from an unrecognised device or browser.	Edit
Login Approvals	Use your phone as an extra layer of security to keep other people from logging in to your account.	Edit
Code Generator	Use your Facebook app to get security codes when you need them.	Edit
App Passwords	Use special passwords to log in to your apps instead of using your Facebook password or Login Approvals codes.	Edit
Public key	Manage an OpenPGP key on your Facebook profile and enable encrypted notifications.	Edit
Your trusted contacts	Choose friends who you can call to help you get back into your account if you are locked out.	Edit
Recognised Devices	Review which browsers you've saved as ones you often use.	Edit
Where You're Logged In	Review and manage where you're currently logged in to Facebook.	Edit
Profile picture login	Manage your Profile picture login settings	Edit
Legacy Contact	Choose a family member or close friend to care for your account if something happens to you.	Edit
Deactivate your account	Choose whether you want to keep your account active or deactivate it.	Edit

Click on the edit button

Deactivate your account

Deactivating your account will disable your Profile and remove your name and photo from most things that you've shared on Facebook. Some information may still be visible to others, such as your name in their Friends list and messages that you've sent. Learn more.

Deactivate your account.

Close

Now click on the Deactivate your tab account.

You will be prompted to enter your password

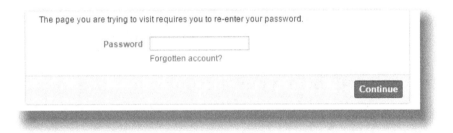

The page you are trying to visit requires you to re-enter your password.

Password [ ]

Forgotten account?

Continue

You will finally be placed on a screen where you should opt out of future emails from Facebook, Uncheck the messenger box and finally deactivate the account

Reason for leaving required	○ This is temporary. I'll be back.
	○ I don't find Facebook useful.
	○ I receive too many emails, invitations and requests from Facebook.
	○ I don't understand how to use Facebook.
	○ I have another Facebook account.
	○ My account was hacked.
	○ I spend too much time using Facebook.
	○ I have a privacy concern.
	○ I don't feel safe on Facebook.
	● Other (please explain further):
Please explain further	
Email opt-out	☑ Opt out of receiving future emails from Facebook
	Even after you've deactivated, your friends can still invite you to events, tag you in photos or ask you to join groups. If you opt out, you will NOT receive these email invitations and notifications from your friends.
Messenger	☐ Keep me signed in to Messenger
	Even if you deactivate your Facebook account, you can still chat on Messenger. Your profile picture will still be visible in your conversations and people will still be able to search for you by name to send you a message. You will continue to appear to friends on Facebook in places where they can message you.

Deactivate   Cancel

Do not log into your account for the next 14 days and your account will be deleted entirely.

Should you log in before the two weeks have elapsed, Facebook will not delete your account and will assume you do not wish to remove it permanently.

It could take approximately 90 days for Facebook to delete everything you ever posted, your photos, videos, status updates and other data stored in the backup systems. Sometimes your old photos may show up in a search so it would be advisable for you to delete every photo on your account manually before you request for your account to be deleted.

You may also follow this link: https://www.facebook.com/help/delete_account to delete your account without deactivating your account first.

Be absolutely sure that you want to delete your account with Facebook as this option has no grace period where you can reactivate your account.

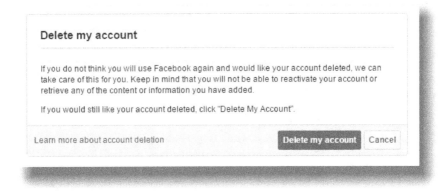

HOW TO PERMANENTLY DELETE A TWITTER ACCOUNT

Twitter is a microblogging site that allows users to stay up to date with current events and trends all around the world. Users post Tweets, which are short instant messages with a limit of up to 140 characters. You can also images and short videos, and GIF's.

You cannot delete your Twitter account from your Android/iPhone app. You must log into a web browser.

Step 1:_Log into your Twitter from a web browser e.g. Chrome, Firefox or Safari on your computer.

Click on your profile tab and click on settings

Step 2: Scroll to the bottom of the **account** tab and click deactivate my account.

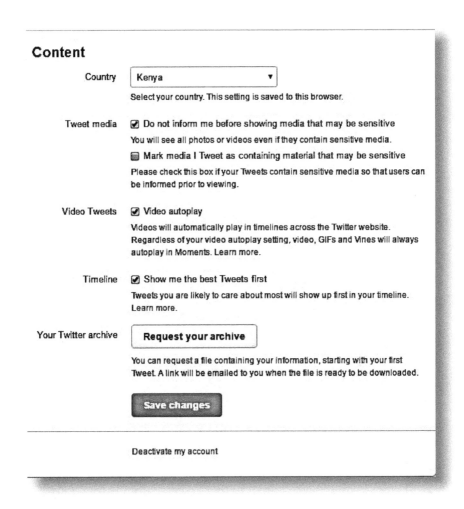

You will be informed about how long the deletion process will take, and other miscellaneous information.

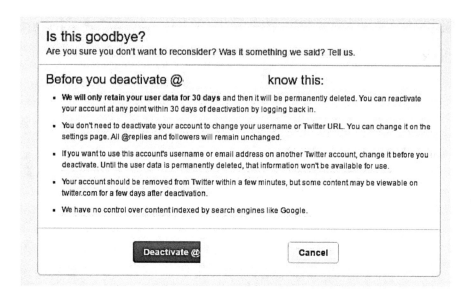

Step 3: It will then ask you to enter your Twitter password for security purposes. Enter your password and then your account will be deactivated.

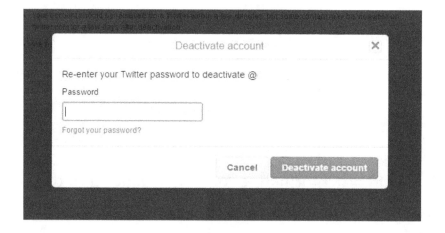

It will take about 30 days to permanently delete your account. This 30 day period is also there just in case you changed your mind and decided to return to Twitter. After the 30 day period, your Twitter account will be permanently deleted.

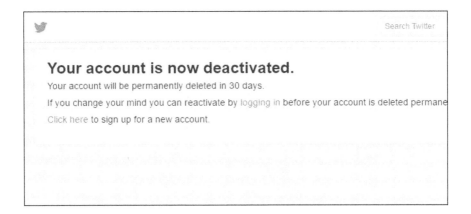

HOW TO PERMANENTLY DELETE AN INSTAGRAM ACCOUNT

Instagram is a popular photo-sharing app that was created in 2011 and now has over 600,000000 subscribers. It became part of the Facebook in 2014. Instagram does not let users delete their accounts directly from the app. For you to delete it, you must log into your Instagram from a web browser.

Step 1

Using a web browser or a mobile web browser, log into your Instagram account.

Step 2

Navigate to this link:

https://instagram.com/accounts/remove/request/permanent/

You are free to give a reason why you would like to delete your Instagram account. Key in your password again and click on the red permanently delete my account button.

HOW TO PERMANENTLY DELETE A LINKEDIN ACCOUNT

LinkedIn is the world's largest and most popular professional networking site, with 400 million users. It helps professionals all over the world connect, share ideas opinions and find opportunities. However, it is still vulnerable to security threats like other networking sites. Note the following after you delete your LinkedIn account:

If your LinkedIn profile was visible on search engines, e.g., Google, Yahoo, or Bing, it could take a while for your LinkedIn information to completely disappear from the search results depending on how the search engines collect and update their search results.

After your LinkedIn account has been closed for 24 hours, any email addresses associated with it will be freed up to use for other new or existing accounts. It should take about 24 hours for you to completely delete your LinkedIn account.

This is how to delete your LinkedIn account:

Step 1: Go to linkedin.com in your web browser and log in.

Step 2: Move your mouse cursor over your profile picture in the top-right corner, and select **Privacy & Settings** from the drop-down menu that appears.

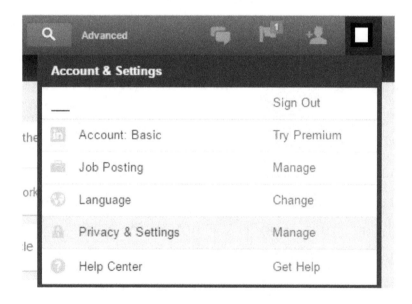

Step 3: In the bottom window, click **Account**, and scroll to the very bottom, then click on **Close Your Account**.

Link, remove, and control visibility of your WeChat account

Basics

Third parties

Subscriptions

Subscriptions

Try Premium for free	Change
Unlock the power of LinkedIn	
Closing your LinkedIn account	Change
Learn about your options, and close your account if you wish	

Go to previous version of Settings

Step 4: On the next screen, LinkedIn will ask you why you want to cancel your LinkedIn account. Click a button beside the reason that most applies to you (if you select "Other," click in the text box that appears and write a few details), and then click **Continue**.

Tell us why you're closing your account:

◯ I have a duplicate account

◯ I'm getting too many emails

◯ I'm not getting any value from my membership

◯ I have a privacy concern

◯ I'm receiving unwanted contact

● Other

Your feedback matters. Is there anything else you'd like us to know?

[text area]

| Back to Settings | Next |

Step 5: LinkedIn will show you details about your account to make sure that it is the one that you wish to remove from LinkedIn. If it is, click **Verify Account**. If it isn't, click **Sign Out** and start again at step 1.

Last step before closing your account...

Closing your account means you lose your profile and all your LinkedIn data.

For your security, enter your password to make this change

Password

☑ Unsubscribe me from LinkedIn email communications, including invitations.

Back to Settings   **Close account**

Step 6: LinkedIn will display a page telling you what happens when you delete your account. If you are certain that you still want to delete your LinkedIn account, click **Close Account**.

REMOVE YOUR EMAIL ACCOUNTS

Your email accounts are attached to a lot of services you would sign up for. This is where a lot of your information online is tied to. Deleting your email address is of vital importance if you want to go off the grid. When you do this, you will have to look for alternative methods of communicating and using services online. We will cover this in another topic.

HOW TO PERMANENTLY DELETE A GMAIL ACCOUNT

When you delete your Gmail account, you will delete all your emails and close your inbox.

Note that Emails will still exist in the email accounts of the people with whom you've communicated with unless they have also deleted their email accounts.

If anyone tries to email you at that address after you've deleted the account, the email will bounce back.

THINGS TO CONSIDER BEFORE DELETING YOUR GMAIL ACCOUNT

3rd Party Access:

You might lose access to 3rd party services associated with your Gmail account. If you use your Gmail account for any other services, you will not be able to access them because the email account is no longer active. Ensure that you update your email address information for those services so as to avoid tricky situations.

For example: If your Gmail account is linked to your bank account. You will have a difficult time trying to access your bank information via email.

Information Loss:

You may lose valuable information if you do not back them up before hitting the delete button.

Deleting your Gmail account does not free up your username:

Nobody else, including you, will ever be able to use your Gmail username in the future. This prevents anybody from trying to impersonate you at your old email account.

Deleting your Gmail account will not delete your Google Account:

Your Google Account will remain associated with things like your search history and YouTube account. You will have to contact the google webmaster to remove your search history. We will look at that later.

STEPS TO DELETE YOUR GMAIL ACCOUNT

Step 1:

Enter your Gmail username or email address and click Sign in. Proceed to click on 'My account' in the top left corner of your Gmail as shown below:

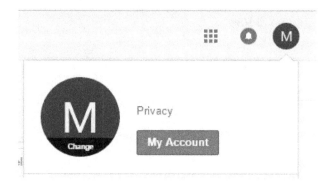

Step 2: Click my account under Account Preferences, click Delete your account or services.

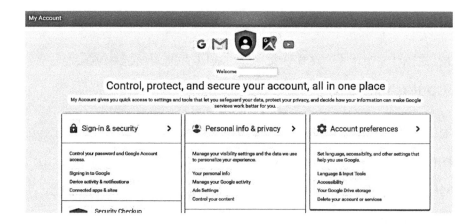

Step 3: Click on Delete Google Account and data.

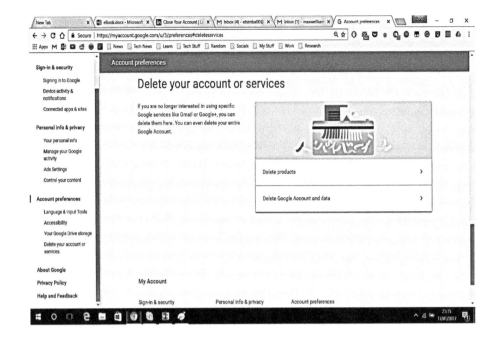

Step 4: Re-enter your password, then click Sign in.

Step 5: Next, you will be asked to confirm if you want to proceed. Read the terms very carefully before proceeding. At this point, you have the option to download all your data which Google holds. You may want to do this for archival purposes.

Read & tick the checkboxes confirming that you would like to proceed to delete your Gmail account.

Please read this carefully. It's not the usual yada yada.

You're trying to delete your Google Account, which provides access to various Google services. You'll no longer be able to use any of those services, and your account and data will be lost.

You also could lose access to services outside of Google where you use your bank account, you may have difficulty resetting your bank password. If you proceed, you'll need to update your email address everywhere you use it outside of Google.

You can download your data before deleting your account.

All this content will be deleted

Note: the list below may not contain every Google service affected by your deletion, such as services Google no longer supports. Your data will be deleted from these services as well.

M   Gmail   386 conversations will be deleted

                                       Most recent: New sign-in from Chrome on Windows
                                       12 minutes ago

If you have any pending financial transactions you will still be responsible for those charges.

☐   Yes, I acknowledge that I am still responsible for any charges incurred due to any pending financial transaction and I understand that under certain circumstances my earnings won't be paid out.

☐   Yes, I want to permanently delete this Google Account and all its data.

DELETE ACCOUNT   CANCEL

Step 6: Once the above steps have been done you should be greeted by this screen:

Google

Your Google Account and all its data have been deleted

If you accidentally deleted your Google Account, you have a
short amount of time to try to recover it:

1. Go to Account support
2. Follow the steps to verify that the account is yours

If for any reason, you feel like undoing this google deletion, you have a very limited time to contact Google Account Support to try and retrieve your account.

HOW TO PERMANENTLY DELETE YOUR YAHOO MAIL ACCOUNT

Yahoo was the biggest free email service provider until Gmail came along. It has had its fair share of data breaches. On December 14, 2016, Yahoo disclosed that hackers had obtained access to more than 1 million Yahoo user accounts in August 2013. This is just one of the few data beaches that Yahoo has experienced. Take charge of your privacy and security by deleting your Yahoo account.

Before you delete your Yahoo Mail account, please note that you will remove access to all of your Yahoo services.

How to delete your Yahoo Mail account

Step 1: Navigate you your yahoo mail and sign in.

After signing in, go to this link:

https://edit.yahoo.com/config/delete_user

Step 2

After verifying that you have entered the correct Yahoo ID and read the account deletion warning, enter your Yahoo password.

We are sorry to see you go!
Are you sure you want to terminate your Yahoo! Account?
If so, please confirm your identity with your password.

Step 3:

Scroll down and enter a visual or visual code. You can request for a new code if you cannot see or hear the current code. Finally, click on Terminate this Account.

Yahoo! Account Terminated

Your account has been deactivated and scheduled for deletion.

You no longer have access to this account, which will be deleted from our user database in approximately 90 days. This delay is necessary to discourage users from engaging in fraudulent activity.

Click here to learn what information may possibly remain in our archived records after your account has been deleted.

Back to Yahoo!

Terms | Privacy

Success! Your Yahoo account has been deleted

DELETE SEARCH ENGINE RESULTS THAT FEATURE YOU

Search engines discover new content online through a process called crawling. This data is then indexed in the search engines servers and stored in massive databases. The indexing process analyses the data and stores the information in these databases. The final process is the retrieval process, where a user can search for something online, and the search engine will churn out results that may be of interest to the user.

Using the most popular search engine in the world – Google, we can filter results using very specific parameters to narrow down on the results we get and hopefully get the information we would like. We will touch on safer, more privacy oriented search engines in the preceding sections of the eBook.

As you search the web for cookie crumbs that identify with you, having knowledge of how to utilize Google search to its maximum potential is vital. When you are looking for information about your name in an URL, search using the tags: URL: *enter your name here*

This will return results which have your name in the URL

If you know the particular site that and want to check if it has any personal data about you, you can query Google or other search engines with:

Site: www.thesiteyouwichtosearch.com your name here

Knowing these tricks will help you narrow down results that contain information about you and get in contact with the webmasters or get Google to take down the links.

In the next section, we will cover how to get Google to take down links and how to contact webmasters of various sites where your privacy is at risk.

HOW TO REMOVE INFORMATION ABOUT YOU FROM A GOOGLE SEARCH

You can ask Google to remove your sensitive personal information, e.g. bank account number, certain images of you, your handwritten signature, or a nude or sexually explicit image or video of you that's been shared without your consent, from Google search results.

WHAT GOOGLE WILL REMOVE

Google will only remove what it deems necessary, so if there is an image of you that you don't wish to see in a Google search, you must contact the webmaster.

If you want to remove a photo, profile link, or web page from Google Search results, you usually need to ask the website owner (webmaster) to remove the information.

WHY CONTACT THE WEBMASTER?

Even if Google deletes the site or image from our search results, the web page still exists and can be found through the URL to the site, social media sharing, or other search engines. Therefore, your best option is to contact the webmaster, who can remove the page entirely.

If a photo or information shows up in Google search results, it just means that the information exists on the Internet and it doesn't mean that Google endorses it.

TIPS FOR CONTACTING WEBMASTERS

Getting a response from a webmaster may take a long time. Here is the best method to email a webmaster to get the most fruitful response.

It is advisable not to be threatening or resentful in your email to the webmasters of the sites in question. Be polite in your correspondence with the webmaster, and you will be able to get more valuable gains in getting your link or content taken down.

As a rule of thumb, when you email the webmaster include all the links you think infringe on your right to privacy and state the reason why you would like to have said links taken down. Do not put the websites integrity or its business practices to question as you many now face resistance on the part of the webmaster who would now begin to feel threatened.

It is advisable to not continuously spam the site owner but to rather spend on diligently crafted polite email, with your reasons as to why you would like the various links taken down. Here is an example of an email I would send to a webmaster.

John Doe
123 Main Street
Any Town, Utah 12345
November, 15th, 2016
(Data Broker Company's name)
(Street/Mailing Address)

Re: Cease from Your List Immediately.

Dear (Data Broker):

This is a CEASE ANF DESIST ORDER to inform you that your actions including but not limited to selling my personal, financial and marital information in violating my privacy at all levels. I have been getting emails, postal mails and phone calls from all various companies and people that possess some very vital personal information about me, it is my understanding and belief that they obtained this information through your company. You are hereby ORDERED TO STOP IMMEDIATELY as these privacy violations are against the law.

I have the right to remain free from these activities as they constitute a violation of my legal right and freedom, and I will pursue any legal remedies available to me if these unlawful activities do no stop.

I hereby notify you and your company by writing (via this letter) that my information is my property. All previous and future agreements made or expressed either directly or indirectly with any third party are hereby rescinded.

You will have 10(Ten) days to reply to this letter in writing, failure to do so may or will act as evidence of negligence, infringement, and violation upon my legal privacy rights.

Sincerely,

(Your Signature)

John Doe

(Your Address)

WHAT IS AND WHY SHOULD WE WORRY ABOUT DATA BROKERS?

I AM sure you have received mail, paper or electronic from companies that either offered you credit, or other services based on your financial and other status or situation. For example, if you have high balance on credit cards, you probably have seen offers from various banks and other lending institutes that are offering you consolidation loans. If you recently went through bankruptcy or other similar crisis then you probably have seen mail regarding new credit card offers from banks that are offering "2nd chance".

How do they know all these information about us? Well they are like private detectives that monitors our activities such as they go through all court records to find out if you have filed bankruptcy, divorce or if there was a lien filled against you or any other legal actions for that matter. But that is not where they stop.

They also collect data like what we buy, how we spend our money, where we go on vacation, what phones we use, what kind of social life we have (thanks to social media). In other words some of these information can be very personal and private. Once they collect enough information about a person, they then create a profile and fill in the rest and make a complete profile which can explain most of our behavior and other habits better than we can explain ourselves.

They know what ethnicity we are, what our sexual orientation is, what if any illness we suffer from specially illness like HIV, Diabetes, hypertension, mental depression or even substance abused. They know what we eat, what type of movies we like, what kind of websites we like to visit, if we are republican or democrat, you name it they know it.

Scary enough? It is really true, 100% true. As shady as this may sound, the entire industry of data brokerage is completely legal. Does that mean we are at the mercy of these data brokers? Well, yes and no. If you don't do anything than yes you are at their mercy. But on the other hand, if you care enough about your privacy, then act and be heard and take action to get yourself out of these data broker's computer data base. It is hard but it can be done.

One valid question is why do these brokers collect your silly data, well think about it, they make money selling your data to interested companies so those companies can target you based on your profile and your preferences, and offer to sell you their products and or services. It is a billion dollar industry and growing every day. Here is a section of an article from Newsweek on this very topic.

"Data brokers are notoriously secretive. Only one, Acxiom, granted Newsweek an interview with a company officer, despite two months of requests to dozens of firms. "A lot of the information, the deals that take place, are proprietary in nature," says Paul Stephens, a director at Privacy Rights Clearinghouse in San Diego, which advocates for consumer rights regarding personal information. "It's hard to tell who's selling what to whom." In fact, it's unknown exactly how many data brokers operate in the United States, because so many keep a low profile. Credible estimates range from 2,500 to 4,000. There are supergiants in the field—Acxiom, Experian. But there are myriad smaller companies that few have heard of: Exact Data, Paramount Lists, Datalogix, Statlistics.

How do data brokers collect information? As you might guess, Web browsing is a bountiful source. What sites you visit, what topics or products you research there, what you buy, even what you post in forums can be turned into an entry in a broker's database. But there are offline sources as well. Public court records are, of course, public. But retail store owners have found they can bring in additional revenue by selling their sales records to broker companies.

The worst that may happen to you in these cases is you'll get junk mail you don't want. But more insidious things can happen when brokers go beyond names and addresses to selling other information, which brokers' clients usually download from a web server. Several years ago a broker named InfoUSA sold a list of 19,000 verified elderly sweepstakes players to a group of experienced scam artists, who stole over $100 million by calling people on the list and pretending to be government or insurance workers who needed bank account information to ensure their pill prescriptions. The New York Times turned up one InfoUSA list whose description read, "These people are gullible. They believe that their luck can change."

That's the looming threat of data brokerage: While many brokers claim, probably honestly, to only provide publicly available information that can be used to verify someone's identity or prevent fraud, there's a fast-growing market for what's called "consumer scores." Instead of a straight list of names, addresses, and other info, a consumer score is a computer-generated number that attempts to predict your likelihood to get sick, or to pay off a debt. Consumer scores are similar to FICO credit scores, but aren't regulated as to what factors can be used and how transparent the score and its contributing factors are to the scored individual."

No matter how private your life is and how much you try to stay under the radar, anyone with a credit card and $25 can find you by going to one of those sites like "People look up, been verified.com, US Search.com or similar sites. Now, to me that is scary, especially after reading about a lady that spoke about how her husband was killed by a person, whom she helped the DA to prosecute, he was sentenced to 25 years to life, but he got out after serving just 18 years and then once he was out he looked her up online by using one of those data brokers, and showed up at her door. She did survive the whole ordeal and lived to tell about it.

Now one thing I will say to some of this broker's defense that some of these companies do have a system where you can opt out from their list. But my question is I didn't ask to be on your list at the first place, so why do I have to go to every one of these brokers and ask to opt out especially when the actual number of brokers are as high 4000 according to Newsweek? I did not ask them to add me, but I now have to ask them to delete me and half of them won't even offer the option upfront for opting out, unless we ask specifically. How wired is that? Live and Learn I guess.

But I made it my mission to delete myself from them and after 6 months of trying I was successful. Don't believe me? Try and see if you can find me, you know my name, it's on the cover of this book, give it a try see if you can find anything on me. You may find similar names but none would match my exact details. I checked and rechecked I know, I even paid 4 of those companies to find me. Funny thing is, most of these companies want you to charge your credit card to find someone, so when I was trying to find myself,

I didn't charge my bank cards instead I used a prepaid visa card that I bought from CVS. Smart huh?

Okay here is a list of some of the bigger data brokers where you can opt-out at.

411.info	Yes	http://wpremove.411.info/
123 People	Yes	http://www.123people.com/page/people-manager
Accutellus.com	Yes	https://www.accutellus.com/opt_out_request.php
Acxiom	Partial	https://isapps.acxiom.com/optout/optout.aspx
American List Counsel (ALC)	Yes	http://www.alc.com/privacy.htm
Ameridex	No	Ameridex PO Box 193061 San Francisco CA 94119
Ancestry.com	Yes	Email customersolutions@ancestry.com
Ancestry.com: Genealogy	No	http://www.genealogy.com/privacy.html#optout
Ancestry.com: Roots Web	Yes	Email customersolutions@ancestry.com
Any Who (AT&T,Intelius)	Yes	http://www.anywho.com/help/privacy
Arrests.org	No	info@arrests.org
BeenVerified	Yes	http://www.beenverified.com/opt-out-instructions
BlockShopper		http://www.blockshopper.com/faq.html#q4
Check Mate LLC	Yes	support@instantcheckmate.com
CIS Nationwide	No	http://cisnationwide.com/optout.html
CIS Nationwide	No	http://www.completebackgroundchecks360.com
CIS: Birth Records	No	http://www.birth-records.com/
CIS: Cell Phone Registry	No	http://cellphoneregistry.com/
CIS: Civil Records.org	No	http://civilrecords.org/
CIS: Court Records	No	http://www.courtrecords.org/lp_optout.php
CIS: Court Registry	No	http://courtregistry.org/index.php?xpath=privacy

Name	Opt-out	URL
CIS: Criminal Records	No	http://www.criminal-records.org/terms.php
CIS: Criminal Registry	No	http://criminalregistry.org/
CIS: Data Detective	No	http://datadetective.com/terms.php
CIS: Death Records	No	http://deathrecords.org/index.php?xpath=lp_optout
CIS: Divorce Records	No	http://www.divorcerecords.org/index.php?xpath=privacy
CIS: Email 411	No	http://email-411.com/index.php?xpath=lp_optout
CIS: Email Tracer	No	http://www.emailtracer.com/tos.php
CIS: eVerify	Yes	http://www.everify.com/legal.php#remove
CIS: Free Background Check	No	http://freebackgroundcheck.us/terms.php
CIS: GovArrestRecords.org	Yes	www.GovArrestRecords.org/opt_out_form.pdf
CIS: Governmentregistry.org	No	http://governmentregistry.org/index.php?xpath=privacy
CIS: GovPoliceRecords.org	Yes	http://www.govpolicerecords.org/opt_out_form.pdf
CIS: Govregistry.us	No	http://govregistry.us/privacy.php
CIS: GovWarrantRecords.org	Yes	http://www.govwarrantrecords.org/index.php?xpath=terms
CIS: Info Pages	No	http://infopages.com/info/terms
CIS: Info Registry	Yes	http://members.inforegistry.com/customer/terms.php
CIS: Intel Registry	Yes	http://intelregistry.com/terms.php
CIS: InteliGator	Yes	http://www.inteligator.com/home/optout.php
CIS: Locate People	No	http://locatepeople.org/index.php?xpath=lp_optout
CIS: Marriage Records	No	http://www.marriagerecords.org/
CIS: People Fact Finder	No	http://www.peoplefactfinder.com/
CIS: People Finder	No	http://www.peoplefinderonline.net/privacy.html
CIS: People Records	Yes	Terms of Service, Section 21
CIS: Phone Registry	No	http://www.phoneregistry.com/privacy.php
CIS: Public Records Checks	No	http://publicrecordschecks.com/privacy.php
CIS: Records	Yes	http://recordsauthority.com/access/optout.php
	Yes	http://members.retrosleuth.com/customer/
	No	

Name	Opt-out	URL
Authority	No	http://www.reversegenie.com/data_optout.php
CIS: Retro Sleuth	No	http://www.reversemobile.com/index.php?xpath=privacy
CIS: Reverse Genie	No	http://reversenumberdatabase.com/terms
CIS: Reverse Mobile	No	http://reversephonecheck.com/privacy.html
CIS: Reverse Number Database	Yes	http://reverserecords.org/index.php?xpath=lp_optout
CIS: Reverse Phone Check	No	http://ssnrecordsearch.com/tos.html
CIS: Reverserecords.org	No	http://www.staterecords.org/index.php?xpath=lp_optout
CIS: Social Security Number Records	No	http://www.stateregistry.org/index.php?xpath=lp_optout
CIS: State Records (United States State Records)	No	
CIS: StateRegistry.org	Yes	http://webinvestigator.org/
CIS: Webinvestigator.org	Yes	http://webstigate.com/index.php?xpath=lp_optout
CIS: Webstigate.com	Yes	http://instantbackgroundreport.com/
Instantbackgroundreport.com	Yes	http://www.peoplefinders.com/optout-form.pdf
Confi-Chek: People Finders	Yes	http://www.peoplefinders.com/manage/
Confi-Chek: Private Eye	No	http://www.publicrecordsnow.com/static/view/privacy
Confi-Chek: Public Records Now	No	http://www.usa-people-search.com/manage/
Confi-chek: USA People Search	Yes	
Confi-Chek: Veromi.com	Yes	http://www.veromi.net/privacy.aspx
Corporation Wiki	No	http://support.corporationwiki.com/entries/21076867-
Criminal Pages	No	http://www.criminalpages.com/optout/
Datalogix	Yes	https://www.datalogix.com/privacy/#opt-out-landing
Detective Unlimited	No	http://www.detectiveunlimited.com/privacy-policy.html
DEX Media (DEX online.com)	No	http://green.dexknows.com/DexGreen/selectDexAction.do
DOB Search	No	https://www.dobsearch.com/faq.php
eBureau	No	http://www.ebureau.com/privacy-center/opt-out
eFind Out the Truth	Yes	http://www.efindoutthetruth.com/disclaimer.htm
	Yes	http://www.employeescreen.com/privacy.asp
	Partial	http://www.enformion.com/help.aspx?vw=statement
	Partial	http://www.epsilon.com/consumer-preference-center
	No	

EmployeeScreenIQ	partial	http://64.129.51.74/epsilon-consumer-preference-center
Enformion, Peoplefinders.com	Yes	www.optoutprescreen.com
Epsilon (Alliance Data)	Yes	http://www.experian.com/privacy/opting_out.html
Epsilon: Abacus	Yes	DataPrivacyOfficer@ldschurch.org
Equifax	Yes	SharingOptOut@FICO.com
Experian	Yes	PSAC@harte-hanks.com
FamilySearch.org	Yes	http://www.archives.com/ga.aspx?_act=Optout
FICO	Yes	http://www.emailfinder.com/EFC.aspx?_act=optout
Harte Hanks	no	http://www.freephonetracer.com/FCPT.aspx?_act=Optout
Inflection: Archives.com	Yes	
Inflection: emailfinder.com	No	http://www.goodhire.com/privacy http://www.peoplesmart.com/?_act=optoutpolicy
Inflection: Freephonetracer.com	Yes	http://www.phonedetective.com/PD.aspx?_act=OptOut
Inflection: Goodhire.com	Yes	http://www.infopay.com/affiliatecenter/terms
Inflection: PeopleSmart	No	http://list.infousa.com/PrivacyPolicyInfo.htm
Inflection: PhoneDetective	Yes	http://www.background.com/terms-of-service/
Info Pay	Yes	optout@instantpeoplefinder.com
InfoGroup: InfoUSA	Yes	https://www.intelius.com/optout.php http://www.networkadvertising.org/choices/
InfoRegistry	Yes	http://www.lookupanyone.com/privacy-faq.php#faq4
Instant People Finder	Yes	http://www.numberinvestigator.com/privacy
Intelius	Yes	https://www.intelius.com/optout.php
Intelius: Addresses.com	Yes	https://www.intelius.com/optout.php
Intelius: LookupAnyone.com	Yes	http://www.phonesbook.com/about.php
Intelius: Numberinvestigator	Yes	http://www.publicrecords.com/privacy
Intelius: People Lookup	Yes	http://www.sverify.com/help.html http://www.unlimitedbackgroundchecks.com/privacy.html
Intelius: Peoplesearches.com	Yes	http://www.ussearch.com/consumer/ala/landing.do?did=538
Intelius: PhonesBook.com	No	
Intelius: Publicrecords.com	Yes	http://www.zabasearch.com/block_re

Company	Opt-out	Opt-out link / contact
Intelius: Sverify.com	Partial	cords/
Intelius	Yes	http://www.jailbase.com/en/opt-out/
Intelius: US Search	yes	info@kgbpeople.com http://www.lexisnexis.com/privacy/directmarketingopt-out.aspx
Intelius: ZabaSearch	Yes	http://www.lexisnexis.com/privacy/for-consumers
Jailbase	No	https://www.peoplewise.com/show/optoutdisclaimer
kgbpeople	Yes	Attn: Circulation, 1716 Locust Street, Des Moines, Iowa 50309
LexisNexis (direct marketing)	Yes	http://mugshots.com/faq.html
LexisNexis: Accurint (Seisint)	No	privacy@mylife.com
LexisNexis: Peoplewise	Yes	http://www.mylife.com/faq.pub
Meredith Corporation	Yes	http://www.openonline.com/Home/About-Us
Mugshots	Yes	http://peeepls.com/privacy-policy.html
MyLife: Wink	Yes	http://www.peekyou.com/about/contact/optout/
MyLife.com	Yes	http://easytolocate.com
OPENOnline	Yes	http://www.peoplesearchnow.com/optout-form.pdf
Peeepls.com	Yes	http://www.peoplefinder.com/optout.php
Peek You	Yes	http://www.whitepages.com/privacy_central#6
People Search	Yes	
People Search Now	No	http://www.phonebooks.com/data.html
People-Finder.com	Yes	http://pipl.com/directory/remove/ http://www.poedit.org/auth/removal_request.html
Phone Book	Yes	
Phonebooks.com	Yes	http://profileengine.com/#/help
pipl	Yes	see #7 on Privacy Policy Says contact customer support
PoEdit	Yes	
Profile Engine	No	http://radaris.com/page/
PublicBackgroundChecks.com	Yes	https://www.rapleaf.com/opt-out/ http://www.reversephonelookup.com/remove.php
Publicrecordssearchonline.org	No	
Radaris	partial	go to Help, people search
RapLeaf	Yes	http://www.spoke.com/privacy
Reverse Phone	Yes	

Lookup	No	http://www.spokeo.com/privacy
Search Bug	Yes	http://www.superpages.com/about/copyright.html
Spoke	Yes	http://www.toppeoplefinder.com/remove.aspx
Spokeo	Yes	http://www.toppeoplesearch.com/remove.aspx
Super Pages	Yes	via www.optoutprescreen.com
Top People Finder	Yes	http://usidentify.com/company/Opt-Out-Form.pdf
Top People Search	Yes	Email Profile-Remove@waatp.com.com
TransUnion	Yes	http://west.thomson.com/pdf/privacy/opt_out_form.pdf
US Identify	Yes	http://www.whitepagescustomers.com/
Waatp		http://www.whitepages.com/help/privacy_central#6
West Law		http://www.whitepages.com/help/privacy_central#6
Whitepages.com		
Whitepages.com: Address.com		http://www.whitepagescustomers.com/
Whitepages.com: Phonenumber.com		https://www.wilanddirect.com/opt-out-policy
Whitepages.com: Switch Board		http://www.kbmg.com/privacy-policy/
Wiland Direct		http://www.i-behavior.com/
WPP: KBM Group		http://www.zoominfo.com/lookupEmail
WPP: KBM Group: iBehavior		
Zoom Info		

(If this list is hard to read, please feel free to send an email to valenciapublishing@gmail.com and ask for the Opt out list and it will be emailed to you in Microsoft Excel format)

REMOVE YOURSELF FROM DATA COLLECTION SITES

Getting yourself removed from these types of sites is notoriously hard, some can blatantly refuse to take down any information about you, sighting that the data they have is "in the public domain." But with a bit of perseverance, it is possible to get yourself erased.

You should search for yourself on these sites. If you happen to find information about yourself on these sites, you can contact them on their contact page, send them an email requesting a takedown. If you don't get a response and you feel that the data that they hold about you infringes your rights you can get in contact with Google to get the links taken down from Google.

CLOSE YOUR PERSONAL SITES

If you own a website or a domain, there is a huge potential for your information to leak. You should consider using privacy tools and safeguards to mask your identity to the public.

CANCEL ALL MAILING LISTS

If you are part of mailing lists, before you delete your email address, you should comb through your inbox and look for these mailing lists that you subscribed to. One by one list and unsubscribe from them. This will ensure that your email and all the personal details that were attached to it such as your name date of birth are not in use and floating out there in the digital sphere, out of your control.

It may seem like a tedious process, but it is well worth it ensures that your data and right to privacy are not infringed upon later by these mailings.

CONSIDER USING A PROFESSIONAL COMPANY TO REMOVE YOUR DETAILS FROM THE INTERNET.

There are professional services online that offer the ability to track, find and get content about you that is online deleted. These are services that are fee-based but are well worth your investment as they will take away all the hustle that comes with erasing your digital footprint.

One premium site is DeleteMe at Abine.com (https://www.abine.com/deleteme/landing.php) they will go through all the major hoops for you, keep you updated on progress and ensure that sites which take down your information don't put it back up months later.

OTHER WEBSITES TO GET YOURSELF DELETED FROM:

Here is a helpful link to help you erase yourself from sites which are notorious for using dark pattern techniques to make it difficult to find and delete your accounts with them. This site lists popular sites and has links to get directly to the account deletion/deactivation pages. It ranks the sites based on difficulty and is a pretty quick and painless process to get accounts off the sites you signed up for pretty fast.

http://backgroundchecks.org/justdeleteme/

PART – 2

HOW TO REMAIN ANONYMOUS ONLINE

14 WAYS TO STAY ANONYMOUS ONLINE

BROWSING the internet has become extremely risky in the last few years. We face so many threats such as hackers trying to steal sensitive personal information, increased surveillance from governments, both local and international. Privacy online has now become a luxury. However, there are still ways to stay safe and keep your anonymity, which we shall examine in detail

USE A PRIVATE BROWSING/INCOGNITO MODE

If you do not have your own personal computer and have to share e.g. with family, friends, etc. or are at a public computer e.g. in a cyber café, switching on private mode stops your browsing history from being stored on the computer. This also prevents the sites you visited from popping up later, e.g. in an auto-completed web address.

Most browsers have tracking protection in private/incognito browsing. This prevents third-party cookies, i.e. Small text files that track your movement between various sites are also blocked, and first-party cookies that track your movement within a site in order to keep track of, e.g. your shopping preferences are deleted at the end of your session, so that the next time someone visits that particular site, there will be no record of you being there.

How to Do This:

Go to the toolbar of your browser and select a private or incognito mode.

ELIMINATE ALL COOKIES

Blocking or deleting third-party cookies stops some tracking, but not all of it. Flash cookies, better known as super cookies, can store much more information and are left by sites that run Flash, which is almost every site with video content. These super cookies can track your movements across different browsers and even restore third-party cookies that you previously deleted. To stop cookies, go to your browser's Privacy settings.

What to Do:

Download the free CCleaner tool to clear both Flash and regular cookies. However, some sites use third-party cookies to track you within the site, so you may find yourself having to sign in constantly.

STOP YOUR BROWSER SENDING LOCATION DATA

Almost all browsers have a feature that sends your geographical location to sites you visit, so as to offer you more relevant, and useful experiences, e.g. An online shopping site automatically knows where you are shopping from, so Google can return with nearby search results. Nonetheless, advertisers or sites can use that exact information to add to that ad profile of you.

What to Do:

Reject location requests from websites that are not necessary. Though the default option is always opt-in, i.e., your browser will ask you the first time a website wants your location, you can also disable the feature completely:

For Chrome – Preferences > Settings > Advanced > Content settings, and choose to either disallow any site to track your physical location, or ask when a site wants to track.

For Safari – Preferences > Privacy, where you can disable location services, or let each website make a request.

For Firefox – Type "about config" in the URL bar, then "geo.enabled." Double-click to disable location entirely. Otherwise, Firefox always asks before sending your location to a website.

For Microsoft Edge – You don't set this using the Edge browser. You'll need to turn off location tracking using your computer's main Settings > Privacy and then scroll down to Choose apps that can use your precise location and toggle Microsoft Edge to Off.

USE ANONYMOUS SEARCH ENGINES

Google, the most popular search engine in the world has more than 75% of global search traffic, with billions of search queries processed every day. It uses this data to provide more personalized search results, which are highly relevant for most of us, on the other hand, it also creates a 'bubble' of you-centric search that could hinder you from seeing particular web pages based on what you have clicked on in the past.

What to Do:

You can turn off Google's personalized search by hitting Search Tools > All Results > Verbatim. However, this does not give complete anonymity. To prevent your searches being tracked, which will affect the ads you are shown switch to a private search engine such as DuckDuckGo.

Stop Google from Tracking You

Due to its vast blend of services, ranging from Gmail, Calendar, Google+, YouTube, Search and many more, Google is able to build a profile of who you are, what you like and what you do online. Its unified privacy policy means that it can track you across all its services that include scanning your email and use the information cross-product to personalize your experience. The advantages could be things like getting location-specific calendar reminders, but the downside is the targeted ads based on your email content or your picture turning up on items you've liked while logged into Google+.

What to Do:

Opt out of "shared endorsement" in ads and turn off ad personalization. You will still be shown ads, but they will not be targeted. Lastly, download the Google Analytics Browser Add-on to stop Google Analytics from using data on your movements to create profiles for its ad partners

STOP SOCIAL SITES FIGURING YOU OUT

It is common knowledge that social networking sites have collected a huge amount of information on us based on what we do within their sites e.g. things we like, people we click on most and what we search for. But then again sites like Facebook, Twitter, and LinkedIn track users even after they've logged out of their accounts.

One way is when you click on social media sharing buttons, such as a Facebook Like button, or a Twitter share button. But even if you don't share content, the very act of visiting a web page that contains such buttons sends the information back to the 'mothership,' which allows advertisers to carry on showing the same ad to someone who has visited their web page and left.

Facebook, which has its own mobile ad network, uses an alternative to a tracker called a conversion pixel that advertisers use to track how many clicks or sales they receive. The information goes back to Facebook, irrespective of whether the advertiser's site had a Facebook button on it.

What to Do:

Go to Facebook's Settings / Adverts to control whether ads are targeted based on your clicks in and out of Facebook; for Twitter, Settings / Security, and Privacy, then uncheck the box for "Tailor ads..." for LinkedIn, Privacy & Settings / Account / Manage Advertising Preferences.

In all of these cases, you will not receive ads based on your browsing, but you'll still be tracked, ostensibly for security reasons. (However, some sites, including Twitter, honor the Do Not Track setting found in your browser's privacy setting, which means they will not log your presence at their site.)

OPT OUT OF TRACKING

All sites on the internet are fixed with tracking cookies in the many pieces of content they contain, e.g. ads, comment boxes, and sponsored links. These cookies are put there by different ad networks that are made up of countless advertisers who get data on what sites you click on within specific ad networks. This data is then used to create a profile that is shared among the members of an ad network so they can target advertising based on your observed preferences and habits.

What to Do:

Go to your browser's privacy settings and turn on Do Not Track. To lessen data collection on your web movements further, you can also opt-out of tracking at Network Advertising Initiative and Digital Advertising Alliance, by any advertisers who are part of these organizations

BLOCK ALL TRACKERS

Opting out can stop you from being tracked by many sites. However many more may not fulfill such requests. Anti-tracker browser plugins can prevent these cookies from monitoring you on the internet.

What to Do:

Download an anti-tracker plugin such as the Electronic Frontier Foundation's Privacy Badger, Ghostery, or Disconnect, which blocks tracking cookies to stop ad analytics companies from creating an extensive profile of just where you like to go on the internet.

DISABLE JAVA AND UNUSED PLUGINS

Plug-ins is downloadable, tiny programs that improve your browser's capabilities, e.g. when playing certain video or animations. Sadly, two of the most commonly required plugins, Adobe Flash and Java, are also to blame for exposing identifying details about your browser.

In particular, Java is well-known to "fingerprint" a browser by displaying to sites a glut of identifying details such as IP address, fonts downloaded and much more.

What to Do:

Because plugins are also an extremely common way for malware to find its way into a browser, it would not be a bad idea to disable them, especially the ones that are rarely used. And, where once the vast lion's share of sites needed Java to run their various animations or interactive pieces, these days gradually more sites are built using code that can be natively run by browsers.

Chrome: Enter "chrome://plugins/" into your search bar. To disable you want to disable them temporarily, just click "Disable."

Firefox: Type "about add-ons" into the search bar, then select Plugins. You can choose to activate the plugins always, never, or only after asking permission.

Safari: Head to Preferences > Security > Plug-in Settings to turn each on or off.

Microsoft Edge: Luckily, this browser has no plugins available to you. If you get messages on certain sites that you need to run these plug-ins, you may want to invest in a script-blocker extension such as NoScript (Firefox) or ScriptNo (Chrome). These halts all Flash and Java by default, with options to build a whitelist of trusted sites that need these plugins.

USE A PROXY NETWORK

All of the above options are excellent for avoiding tracking cookies that can give marketers what they need to create astoundingly detailed profiles of who you are. But you can still be tracked and identified through the IP address of your browser. IP addresses can identify your fairly accurate location, as well as how often you visit certain sites.

To salvage a little more anonymity, a virtual private network (VPN) disguises your IP address and reallocates you a new one, so that you appear to be surfing from a separate location. Each time you log into the VPN, you get a new IP address, preventing people e.g. employer, ISP, etc. from checking what websites you visit.

What to Do:

There are lots of free VPNs available for you to download. However, if you want a faster connection, you should use premium VPN's that are billed monthly. Using a VPN is also a valuable way to protect your data on public Wi-Fi networks.

DOWNLOAD A PRIVATE, ANONYMOUS BROWSER

Plugins, proxies and remembering to turn on private browsing can make for a difficult web experience. If you are ready to give up the comfort of your favorite browser, you can download a whole new browser that offers all of the above features including the ability to turn on a proxy network through a switch in the toolbar.

The Epic browser is grounded on the Chrome browser but with privacy settings dialed up so that third-party cookies are automatically blocked, search and browsing history is never stored, and trackers are always blocked. You will still see ads; however, you will not be tracked, and the homepage displays a captivating counter showing how many trackers tried to log your movements each day.

What to Do:

Get Epic Privacy Browser. Privacy doesn't come at the expense of convenience you can allow auto-fill to complete web forms with previously entered data and although passwords can't be saved within your accounts' sign-in forms, you can download a password extension that does the work for you.

GO COMPLETELY ANONYMOUS WITH TOR

For the greatest level of anonymity, download the TOR browser, which dispenses your internet traffic through a network of TOR servers (nodes) so that a website you visited can view only the IP address of the existing node. Using TOR makes it extremely difficult for anyone to trail you. However, it may slow down your browsing. It can be used for any kind of browsing that requires privacy and security, including visits to sites on the dark web that is not accessible by regular browsers. Whereas these sites mostly tend towards illegal activity and products, safe havens for whistleblowers and political dissidents also exist, and TOR is one of the only ways they can be accessed.

USE DIGITAL CURRENCY

Making purchases online is an easy way to link your identity to specific profiles and websites in spite of everything, you are using your credit card details. If you do not want certain purchases linked with a profile e.g., You may have subscribed to something unorthodox like porn you should consider using a digital currency like Bitcoin, which, like cash, is not linked to any identifying details about you.

Still, because bitcoin transactions are public, a snooper with a mission can track specific amounts to eventually create a profile about who is spending it and link it back to an individual. In the end, staying anonymous online takes tremendous effort tech giants, and service providers go to great lengths to make it incredibly convenient and easy for us to show our movements and profiles in exchange for a free service. Though there are benefits to being tracked, possibly the main concern today is for people to realize that not only are free services costing us our privacy but that our information is so valuable and we should question every company that requests it, invisible or not.

One big question on the minds of a lot of internet users today is one of privacy – just how private is what you do online? How much can be traced back to you? It's an alarming reality, but the answer is honestly, just about everything. It doesn't matter if you're on a public or private Wi-Fi network, at home or at the cafe, your web traffic is linked to your device, which is linked to you.

Most of us are up to pretty innocent antics online, and are just creeped out by the idea that someone is tracing our activity, so who is using that information? What information are they even getting? Is there a way to put a stop to it?

The internet is a big pool of users, but everyone leaves their mark, and unless you take some special measures, everyone from hackers to the NSA will be able to spy on your activity.

VIRTUAL PRIVATE NETWORKS

How can my activity be traced back to me?

Your activity can be traced back to you through your devices IP address. An IP address is a unique code associated with any network-enabled device, and it gives servers your approximate geographic location. Each time you access a website or online service, your IP address must pass through those servers.

Most of the time, this information is used to tell servers details such as what language to display your content in, what content you have access to, and even display some targeted advertisements.

Nonetheless, if you are on sites that have a habit of getting more surveillance from law enforcement, e.g. like BitTorrent or pornographic sites, your IP address can actually be used to trace your activity back to you.

Unless you use a VPN, you are at risk of being tracked by someone, and they may build a profile on everything you have done online and link it back to you.

How Does a VPN Work?

VPNs are services that are created to hide your IP address from hackers, servers, and government surveillance. With a VPN, you can access blocked content, browse anonymously, and protect your data and yourself from hackers.

How it works:

1. Download the software and apps onto your device
2. Select a server location, and connect.
3. Your IP address is hidden, and you are given the one that is linked to the server you've selected.
4. Your web traffic is also completely encrypted, so you can safely use public networks.

Thus, when you use a VPN, your real IP address is totally undetectable, and you are able to browse online completely anonymously.

WHAT TO LOOK FOR IN A VPN

VPNs have standard features that anyone can use; nevertheless, it is helpful to know how they work, so you know what to look for. Look out for the following:

- **Bandwidth** – These are the data transfer limits imposed by both your internet service provider and the VPN you choose. Most VPNs come with unlimited bandwidth.

- **Multiple connections** – Can you connect multiple devices to the VPN at once? It is nice to be able to use at least two devices on one account; this helps you protect your privacy at home and on other devices.

- **Encryption** – There are two basic strengths of encryption that are used – 128 and 256 bit. The latter of the two is the strongest and highly recommended. Also, choose a VPN that allows you to select your own security protocol.

Encryption may slow down your connection. You should be able to choose how strong you would like your encryption to be, so you can optimize your connection for either speed or security, depending on what you are doing.

- **Network** – The size of a VPN's network can significantly affect the speed of your connection, make sure you use a VPN with at least 50 servers within their network. The more servers there are, the wider the distribution of users you will get, and the more available bandwidth.
- **System Compatibility** – Ensure the VPN is compatible with all of your devices. Most VPNs are compatible with at least Windows and Mac, but you would most likely want one that works on mobile devices as well.

Apart from these things, you will want to look for a VPN that is easy to use, with automatic setup, and excellent customer service just in case you may need some help. Make sure they are available 24/7, and that there is a direct way to get in touch with them, e.g. live chat.

Now let's take a look at the most popular Android apps to browse anonymously.

15 MOST POPULAR ANDROID APPS YOU CAN BROWSE ANONYMOUSLY

1. HOTSPOT SHIELD VPN PROXY

BESIDES traditional features found in almost every VPN app, it also offers banking-level HTTPS encryption to secure the Wi-Fi connection so that the outgoing data can be safeguarded from eavesdroppers.

2. SecureLine VPN

It is created by Avast which is known for creating one of the best antivirus programs in the world. The private VPN Tunnel of SecureLine VPN encrypts the data using an IPsec protocol which makes it very difficult for hackers to snip the data through public Wi-Fi hotspots.

3. SPOTFLUX VPN

Spotflux is a VPN app which protects the privacy of data by giving two levels of protection and decreases the usage of bandwidth by compressing data.

4. HOLA FREE VPN

Hola Free VPN app is mostly for people who are looking for a completely free VPN Android App with remarkable features. Besides securing data and providing access to geographically blocked content, Hola Free VPN also speeds up browsing by choosing and connecting to the nearest and fastest servers automatically from the list of servers located in 190+ countries.

5. SPEED VPN

Speed VPN is an app which allows you to connect to the Internet through servers located at numerous geographical locations. It is designed specifically for web browsing by unblocking geographically restricted sites and viewing of low-resolution videos. Each session of Speed VPN lasts for 60 minutes.

6. SUPER VPN

Super VPN is an incredibly easy Android app to use. It encrypts the traffic to keep the outgoing and incoming data safe from 3rd party tracking without having to register or configure the settings of the device in any particular way.

7. HIDEMAN VPN

The key feature of this VPN is to secure the outgoing data as much as possible and for this to work it uses a 256-bit encryption key algorithm. This muddles up the original data in such a way that if someone is monitoring the data, they would not be able to understand it without the key. The app, however, offers five free hours per week although premium hours can be earned via in-app ad networks.

8. TOUCH VPN

This VPN encrypts data by using Secure Socket Layer (SSL) which keeps a secure and encrypted link between server and client. The app also helps preserve the battery of the device as compared to other VPN Apps.

9. FLASH VPN PROXY

The Flash VPN Proxy app provides a secure and encrypted VPN network to make sure that all your incoming and outgoing data remains intact from hackers and other dangerous people. The greatest thing about it is that you can use it with no problem because as it offers a reasonable amount of bandwidth for communication, which is mostly offered by premium apps. Also, there is no limit to how long you can connect for.

10. CYBERGHOST

CyberGhost is an app that provides banking-level security. Typically people have concerns that the apps might access their personal information that is available on the device, CyberGhost upholds the privacy of its users and does not access any personal information. The free version of the app provides access to 23 servers located in 15 countries, and the premium version gives access to 300 servers in 23 countries.

11. Tigervpns Android VPN

One-Click Android VPN is an app to protect your privacy and hide the source IP address. It offers up to 500MB of free trail traffic upon signing up.

12. MOBIPROXY

This is another useful VPN app to be able to access region-based restricted websites without being tracked. It provides additional security for outgoing and incoming data.

13. PSIPHON

Psiphon provides a simpler way to access everything available on the Internet easily with secure VPN tunnel. A user can also clearly define whether to tunnel everything or just the web browser.

14. ZERO VPN

Zero VPN is an app which lets you use VPN services at no cost with no difficulty. The interface is easy to use which enables in surfing the Internet anonymously.

15. VPN MASTER

VPN Master is also one of the top VPN apps for anonymous Internet usage that does not require any registration. It also allows you to choose any server in America, Europe or Asia with 99.9% uptime.

HOW TO USE TOR FOR WINDOWS

Computer requirements: You must have an internet connection, a computer running Windows 7 or higher. However, it is best to use Windows 8 or higher. This software is free and will take approximately 15 to 30 minutes to install.

WHAT IS TOR?

Tor is an acronym for The Onion Router. It is a voluntary run service that provides both privacy and anonymity online by concealing who you really are and where you are connecting from. This service also protects you from the Tor network itself. For those who may need regular anonymity and privacy when accessing websites, Tor Browser provides a fast and simple way to use the Tor network.

The Tor Browser works just like other web browsers, only that it sends your communications through Tor, making it harder for people who are watching you to know exactly what you are doing online, and more difficult for people monitoring the sites you use to know the exact location where you're connecting from. Bear in mind that only activities you do inside of

Tor Browser itself will be kept hidden. Having Tor Browser installed on your computer does not make things you do on the same computer using other software e.g. your regular web browser anonymous.

WHERE CAN I FIND TOR BROWSER?

Use a browser like Mozilla Firefox, Google Chrome, Microsoft Internet Explorer, or Microsoft Edge and go to https://www.torproject.org/projects/torbrowser.html.en If you are using a search engine to look for the Tor Browser, make sure that the URL is correct.

Do not use any other source, and if you are prompted to accept alternative HTTPS(SSL/TLS) security certificates, do not continue, they are not secure connections. Click the large Download button, or scroll down to the Tor Browser Downloads section. Click on the language of your choice and OS version (Windows 32/64-bit). Some browsers may ask you to authorize whether you want to download this file. Internet Explorer 11 shows a bar at the bottom of the browser window. For any browser, it is best to save the file first before continuing. Click the Save button.

This example shows Tor Browser version 5.0.3. There may be a newer version of Tor Browser available for download. Please download and use the latest version that Tor Project provides.

HOW TO INSTALL TOR BROWSER

Once the download is complete, there may be an option to open the folder where the file was downloaded to. The default location is the Downloads folder. Double-click on the file "torbrowser-install-5.0.3_en-US.exe".

After double-clicking on the Tor Browser installer, a window will then open with a warning about the origin of the software. You must always take these warnings seriously and make sure that you trust the software you want to install and that you got an authentic copy from the official site via a secure connection. Since you know what you want, and you know where to get the software, and the download was from the Tor Project's secure HTTPS site, you may proceed and click Run.

A small window will then open asking what language you would like to use for the Tor Browser. There are quite a few to choose from. Select the language you want and click the OK button.

You will find a new window that will tell you where the Tor Browser will be installed. The default location is your desktop. You may change this to be a different location if you want, but as for now keep the default.

The installation process is finished when you see a window that says you have completed the installation process. If you click the Finish button, the Tor Browser will start right away and "Start Tor Browser" shortcuts will be added to the Start Menu and Desktop.

USING TOR BROWSER

The first time Tor Browser starts, you will get a window that allows you to adjust some settings if necessary. You may have to come back and modify some configuration settings, but you may go ahead and try to connect to the Tor network by clicking the Connect button.

A new window will then open with a green bar that shows Tor Browser connecting to the Tor network.

The first time Tor Browser starts it may take a bit longer than usual, but be patient, and within a minute or two Tor Browser will open and congratulating you.

Click on the Tor Onion logo in the upper left of Tor Browser then the Privacy and Security Settings.

Some features of a normal web browser could make you vulnerable to certain attacks. Other features earlier had bugs in them that revealed users' identities. Turning the security slider to a high setting disables these features.

This will make you safer from sophisticated attackers who could interfere with your Internet connection or use new unknown bugs in these features. Unluckily, turning off these features can make some websites unusable. The default low setting is fine for daily privacy protection, but you can set it to high if you are worried about experienced attackers, or if you do not mind if some websites do not display correctly.

https://ssd.eff.org/en/module/how-use-tor-windows

HOW TO: USE TOR ON MAC OS X

THIS is a guide that explains how to use the Tor Browser on OS X.

- You must have an internet connection and a computer that runs on a new version of MAC OS X

- It is fairly easy to install and will take approximately 150 to 30 minutes.

GETTING TOR BROWSER

Use a browser like Mozilla Firefox or Safari and type: https://www.torproject.org/download/download-easy.html.en in the URL bar. If you are using a search engine to look for the Tor Browser Bundle, ensure that the URL is correct.

Click on the big purple download button to get the installation program for Tor Browser.

The website will then have detected your operating system, and you will get the correct file for OS X. If this does not work, you can click the link to the side of the purple button to download the correct version.

If you are using Safari, the Tor Browser will start to download. In Firefox, you will be asked whether you want to open or save the file. It is always best to save the file, so click the Save button. This example Tor Browser Bundle Version 4.0.8. Check if there is a new version available.

INSTALLING TOR BROWSER

Once the download is complete, you may get an option to open the folder where the file was downloaded to. The default location is the Downloads folder. Double-click on the file Torbrowser-4.0.8-osx32_en-US.dmg. A window will then open asking you to install Tor Browser Bundle by dragging it to your applications folder. You may do so now.

Tor Browser is now installed in your applications folder.

USING TOR BROWSER

To open Tor Browser for the first time, locate it in the finder or in Launchpad on newer versions of OS X.

After clicking on the Tor Browser icon, a window will then open with a warning about the origin of the software. Just like other operating systems, you must always take these warnings seriously and make sure you trust the software that you want to install and that you got an authentic copy from the official site over a secure connection. Since you know what you want, and you know where to get the software, and the download was from the Tor Project's secure HTTPS site, click Open.

The first time Tor Browser starts, you will get a window that allows you to change some settings if necessary. You may have to come back and change some configuration settings, but you can go ahead and connect to the Tor network by clicking the Connect button.

After clicking "Connect," a new window will then open with a green bar that will get longer as the Tor software starts up. The first time Tor Browser starts it may take a bit longer than usual, but within a few minutes Tor Browser should be ready, and a web browser will open congratulating you.

You could verify that you are connected to the Tor network by visiting check.torproject.org. If you are connected the website, it will say "Congratulations. This browser is configured to use Tor."

You can now browse the internet anonymously with Tor.

11 DO'S AND DON'TS OF TOR NETWORK

TOR is one of the best browsers for keeping our anonymity in this day and age of mass surveillance and almost no privacy on the internet. However, Tor cannot completely guarantee your privacy and security if you are not concerned enough. You have to make sure you use it correctly so that you can maintain your privacy. In the same manner, you also need to know and understand Tor's usage tips and guidelines to keep your privacy and security in complete control.

1. DO USE TOR

Anybody who is concerned about their online privacy must never trust the people at the back of the Internet such as Internet service providers, government agencies, web service providers, etc. Tor network is known for providing online anonymity, and that is the main reason why you should use it.

Tor can be used for many kinds of sensitive browsing including, but not limited to, reporting abuse or corruption; serious business activities; inter-state or inter-country communications; publishing anonymous posts; sharing personal secrets with family and friends, etc.

2. DON'T USE WINDOWS

Windows is just not the best choice of operating system to use Tor in an attempt to improve your Internet privacy because of the security bugs, and vulnerabilities present in the system could compromise your privac**y**, even when using Tor.

That is why you should not be browsing websites through Tor on Windows systems. You could consider using Tor-configured Linux systems like Tails and Whonix, or you may set up Tor on any of your favorite Linux operating systems.

3. DO UPDATE YOUR SYSTEM

Tor is simply a software which runs on top of your operating system, which means that Tor is only as safe and secure as the system running Tor. You should frequently update Tor client, Tor-secured applications i.e. browsers, instant messaging clients, email clients, etc., and your computers operating system.

If an attacker is able to get hold of your computer's operating system, then even running Tor can't protect you or your digital communications. Always make sure that your system up-to-date for Tor usage.

4. DON'T USE HTTP WEBSITES

The Onion Router, as the name suggests, is just a traffic router and not a tool to encrypt the network traffic throughout the Internet. That means Tor anonymizes the origin of your network traffic and encrypts everything inside the Tor network, but it does not encrypt your Internet traffic outside the network.

This infers that the exit nodes of the Tor network can read your Internet traffic if it is not in the form of plain unencrypted data. That is why you must always use end-to-end encryption such as SSL or TLS when doing sensitive online communications, and that requires you to use HTTPS websites.

You should also consider using add-ons such as HTTPS everywhere to automatically switch to HTTPS-mode browsing for supported websites.

5. DO ENCRYPT YOUR DATA STORAGE

Tor does anonymize your Internet traffic's origin location, but it does not secure the digital data on your computer. Security the data on your computer can only be done when the information is encrypted using strong cryptographic algorithms.

LUKS or TrueCrypt are examples of encryption that can be used to encrypt your data to protect you from various threats. LUKS offers a reasonably safe data protection on Linux systems while TrueCrypt also proves to be handy in protecting your data.

6. DON'T USE TOR BROWSER

Tor Browser should not be used to protect your online privacy and security. The FBI recently took down freedom hosting, which was another anonymous hosting website that was running as a hidden service on the Tor network. This exposes some vulnerabilities in the Tor browser.

7. DO DISABLE JAVASCRIPT, FLASH, AND JAVA

Tor cannot protect your data with active content such as JavaScript, Adobe Flash, Java, QuickTime, ActiveX controls, VBScripts, etc. because these binary applications run with your user account's privileges, and can access and share your data.

JavaScript is a strong browser language which websites can use to trail you in ways that are not possible to protect using Tor. Java and Adobe Flash run in virtual machines which can ignore your system's configured proxy settings, and therefore bypass Tor's protection and share your data directly with the websites.

Also, they could even store cookies and site's data separately from the browser and operating system, which can be hard to detect and delete. By disabling these technologies in your system using Tor, you may achieve a greater level of protection.

8. DO NOT USE P2P

P2P is not wanted in Tor network because it is just not built for peer-to-peer file sharing. Exit nodes of the network are set up to block file sharing traffic. You may abuse Tor network if you download torrents and it slows down other users' browsing. Furthermore, using Tor with BitTorrent is not secure and is a threat to your online anonymity.

Because of the insecure design of BitTorrent clients, using Tor with them does not make you anonymous because those clients send your IP address directly to the tracker and other peers, thus compromising your anonymity.

9. DO DELETE COOKIES AND SITE'S LOCAL DATA

Tor routes your network traffic through many relays in order to protect you from traffic analysis. It hides your real identity from the websites using network packets to prevent them from gathering data about you. But websites may use workarounds such as cookies and local data storage to trace your online activities, analyze your Internet usage, and detect your real identity.

That is why; you should always cut cookies and site local data while using Tor to protect your privacy. You should also consider using an add-on such as Self-Destructing Cookies to automatically delete cookies.

10. DO NOT USE YOUR REAL EMAIL

You must never use your real email on websites while using Tor. Tor is used to protect online privacy and hide real identity. You cannot hide your real identity if you are giving out your real email on the websites.

If you are really privacy-conscious and do not want to leave your footprint anywhere on the Internet while using Tor, then you must consider a virtual identity which includes no identical information from your original, real-world identity.

11. DO NOT USE GOOGLE

You must not use Google to search the Internet if you care about your privacy. Google is known for collecting information on users' browsing and search history to assist the growth of its ads revenue.

You must consider using alternatives such as Startpage and DuckDuckGo. These services offer search results without logging your IP address and storing cookies on your computer. In simple words, these search engines value your privacy and anonymity, and that is why you must use them while using Tor and keep your anonymity which we shall examine in detail

www.ingramcontent.com/pod-product-compliance
Lightning Source LLC
LaVergne TN
LVHW052306060326
832902LV00021B/3726